"BETWEEN THE SACRED AND THE PROFANE: FIVE PERSPECTIVES ON VARIOUS SUBJECTS SUCH AS: GOD, DEMONS, RELIGION, AND LOVE…

Four friends meet at a bar table to discuss various topics related to their work and diverse knowledge.

Certainly! It seems that these four friends have an interesting combination of professions and diverse knowledge. Let's take a look:

Antônio is a doctor. He likely has extensive knowledge in health, diagnosis, and disease treatment.

João Fernandes is a chemical engineer. He should be familiar with chemical processes, reactions, and materials.

André Augusto is an evangelical pastor. As a religious leader, he may have theological and spiritual knowledge.

Mário is a math and physics teacher. He specializes in logic, calculations, and physical phenomena. Together, these friends can engage in fascinating conversations about medicine, engineering, faith, and science!

Antônio, the doctor, asked: **"What is God to each of you?"**

For each friend, God may have different meanings:

Antônio (the doctor): For him, God can be seen as the creator of the human body, the force that sustains life, and the source of healing. Perhaps he views God through the lens of science and medicine.

João Fernandes (the chemical engineer): João might interpret God as the great architect of the universe, applying chemical and physical principles to understand creation. He may see God in the order and complexity of chemical reactions.

André Augusto (the evangelical pastor): André sees God as the center of his faith and spirituality. He views God as a personal, loving, and transcendent being based on scriptures and religious teachings.

Mário (the math and physics teacher): Mário approaches God more rationally, seeking mathematical patterns and physical laws that govern the universe. He sees God as the underlying harmony in all things.

Ultimately, the perception of God is deeply personal and can vary widely based on individual experiences, beliefs, and perspectives. Each of these friends may have a unique and meaningful view of God. While discussing, Gérson the waiter chimed in: "To me, God is powerful—capable of creating and destroying everything, manipulating space, time, energy, and matter. Immortal, omnipotent, omnipresent, and omniscient."

"Well," Mario responded, thoughtfully stroking his chin, "that's quite a philosophical answer." Gérson smiled and replied, "Indeed, Mario. Everyone has their own interpretation of God. Some see God exactly as you described, while others perceive God as a force of nature, a feeling of love, or even life itself. The beauty of faith lies in its personal and unique nature for each of us. Ultimately, what matters is that this faith brings us peace and makes us better people."

"I'm glad you liked my response," Gérson continued. "Philosophizing while working helps me pass the time, think, and better understand the world and people. Philosophy, like mathematics, physics, medicine, chemistry, and religion, is an art form."

João Fernandes chimed in, intrigued: "Gérson, you're quite the philosopher. Do you know the origin of the word 'philosophy' and its meaning?"

Gérson replied, "Certainly, João Fernandes. The word 'philosophy' comes from Greek and means 'love of wisdom.' A philosopher seeks knowledge for the sake of knowledge, not content with appearances or opinions. A philosopher is an eternal learner who acknowledges their ignorance and curiosity."

Mario then shifted the conversation: **"Now that we've defined God, how about demons—the embodiment of evil?** What are your viewpoints on that?" Antônio, the doctor, responds: "As a physician, I see evil as illness and suffering. It's not an entity but a condition that affects people's health and well-being."

João Fernandes, the chemical engineer, says: "To me, evil is like a harmful chemical reaction. It's the result of components that, when combined, cause damage or destruction."

André Augusto, the evangelical pastor, shares: "In my faith, demons are seen as the personification of evil and temptation. They are a force opposing God, seeking to divert people from the path of righteousness."

Mario, the math and physics teacher, reflects: "From a scientific standpoint, evil isn't a physical entity. However, metaphorically, it can be compared to a complex mathematical problem or a destructive physical phenomenon."

Gérson, with a smile on his face, responds: "Well, Mario, to me, demons were archangel soldiers and angels of God, created to defend all of creation. But the question is, defend against what? I think something might have contaminated them like a virus during their work, transforming them into the destructive demons they are now. They appear in various cultures on our planet and are named based on their specialization."

Belzebub, the Lord of Flies, oversees the corridors where tormented souls struggle in agony. He laughs, his black wings rustling like dry leaves in the wind.

Lilith, the Queen of Serpents, weaves illusions to confuse the unwary. Her hypnotic eyes gleam as she whispers lies into mortal minds.

Asmodeus, the Tempter, is busy at his forge. He shapes chains of suffering, each link representing a committed sin. The intense heat doesn't faze him; he laughs and continues his work.

Mammon, the Lord of Greed, counts gold coins in his chamber. He accumulates wealth stolen from lost souls. His laughter echoes off the stone walls.

And so, in the heart of darkness, demons work tirelessly. There is no rest, only the perpetuation of torment. Their luck lies not in finding treasure but in discovering purpose within the shadows. 🔥👹

In the eternal battle between light and darkness, demons strive to tempt human souls. Allow me to depict scenes illustrating these moments of temptation:

Seduction: A demon whispers sweet words into the ear of a lonely man. It offers riches, power, and worldly pleasures in exchange for loyalty. The man hesitates, gazing into the abyss of temptation.

Doubt: A woman stands at a crossroads, unsure which path to take. A demon disguised as a friend offers deceptive advice. She looks to the sky, seeking divine guidance.

Anger: A wounded, weary young warrior faces a demon in a mental battle. The demon stokes his rage, promising vengeance against his enemies. The warrior struggles to maintain his sanity.

Greed: An ambitious trader is visited by a demon in his business chamber. The demon offers unimaginable profits in exchange for his soul. The trader looks at his family, torn between desire and responsibility.

Loneliness: An elderly woman, sitting on a park bench, is approached by a demon disguised as a deceased relative. It promises companionship and comfort, but the woman senses the coldness of deception.

André raises a new question: **"What is religion to you?"**

Antônio responds with conviction: "To me, religion is a way to connect with God, follow His commandments, and live a life of faith and love. I am Catholic and believe that Jesus Christ is the Son of God, who died on the cross for our sins and rose on the third day. I also believe in the Holy Trinity, the Virgin Mary, saints, angels, and demons." 🧑‍🦳❤️▢

"For me, religion is a way to understand the world, to seek answers to life's big questions, and to find meaning and purpose. João Fernandes responds thoughtfully. I am agnostic, and I'm not sure if there is a God or not, but I respect all religious beliefs and traditions. I'm also interested in philosophy, science, art, and culture, and I believe all these areas contribute to our knowledge and development.

For me, religion is a way to be freed from sin, to repent and convert, to receive God's grace and salvation. André Augusto responds fervently. I am evangelical, and I believe that the Bible is the word of God, which we should faithfully follow. I also believe that Jesus Christ is the only way to God, and we should preach the gospel to all creatures so that everyone can be saved.

For me, religion is a way to deceive oneself, to be misled and alienated, to submit to dogmas and authorities, and to distance oneself from reason and reality. Mario responds ironically. I am an atheist and do not believe in any God or other supernatural entities. I also believe that religion is a human invention used to manipulate the masses, justify wars and violence, and hinder progress and freedom.

The waiter Gérson looked up at the ceiling for a moment and replied to me that all the world's religions are valid; basically, there is one or more powerful beings (God or Gods) based on faith in sacred scriptures, where absolute truths are found. In the end, they all show the same path with some **different dogmas,** which do not help unite various nations and instead cause conflicts, wars, and prejudices.

Mario looked at Gérson and said, "So you're just like me, believing in everything."

"No," replied Gérson. "I truly believe in a higher being, namely God. I'm just saying that all the world's religions converge on the powerful being that creates everything; the rest are stories and dogmas." André Augusto, the evangelical pastor, looked at the others with inquisitive eyes and asked, **"What does fear mean to you?"**

This question from André invites us to explore the theme of fear from different perspectives. Let's enrich the text with facts, emotions, and hypotheses:

Facts about Fear: Fear is a natural response of our nervous system to perceived threatening situations. It triggers physical and emotional reactions, such as increased heart rate and sweating.

There are different types of fear, including real fear (in the face of actual dangers) and imaginary fear (based on assumptions or unfounded concerns).

Fear can be adaptive, alerting us to real dangers, but it can also be debilitating when excessive or irrational.

Emotions Associated with Fear: Fear is often linked to anxiety, which is persistent and anticipatory worry about future events.

The feeling of vulnerability and helplessness accompanies fear, as we feel at the mercy of circumstances.

Hypotheses and Reflections:

André may be seeking to understand how people cope with fear in their lives.
His question may reveal his pastoral concern in helping the faithful deal with their fears.
Perhaps he is reflecting on how faith and spirituality influence our approach to fear.
In summary, André's question invites us to explore fear as a complex human experience that goes beyond a simple concept. ✺

Antônio, the doctor, scratched his beard thoughtfully. "To me, fear is like an unknown disease. Something that hides in the shadows, lurking in our souls. It's like a rare and frightening diagnosis that needs to be treated with caution." Antônio's reflection leads us to delve deeper into the complexity of fear and its implications. Let's explore further!"

Fear is a natural response of our nervous system to situations perceived as threatening. It triggers a cascade of physical and emotional reactions, such as an increased heart rate, sweating, and muscle tension. There are different types of fear, such as real fear (in the face of actual dangers) and imaginary fear (based on assumptions or unfounded concerns). Fear can be adaptive, alerting us to real dangers, but it can also be debilitating when excessive or irrational.

Emotions Associated with Fear: Fear is often linked to anxiety, which is persistent and anticipatory worry about future events.

The feeling of vulnerability and helplessness accompanies fear, as we feel at the mercy of circumstances.

Hypotheses and Reflections:

Antônio may be comparing fear to an "unknown disease" to emphasize its mysterious and unpredictable nature.

The metaphor of fear "hidden in the shadows" suggests that it is present but not fully visible, like an invisible threat.

The "rare and frightening diagnosis" may represent the difficulty in understanding and treating fear, especially when it takes atypical forms. In summary, Antônio invites us to consider fear as something complex and worthy of attention. He reminds us that, just as a doctor investigates a rare disease, we should approach fear with caution and understanding. ✸

João Fernandes, the chemical engineer, crossed his arms, his expression serious. "Fear is like an unpredictable chemical reaction. Sometimes, it's a sudden explosion; other times, it's a slow and insidious corrosion. We need to decipher its components to neutralize it." João's analogy between fear and a chemical reaction leads us to explore this complex emotion from a new perspective. Let's enrich the text with facts, emotions, and hypotheses: Facts about Fear:

Fear is a natural response of our nervous system to situations perceived as threatening. It triggers physical and emotional reactions, such as an increased heart rate and sweating.

The intensity of fear can vary, as well as the speed with which it manifests.

Emotions Associated with Fear: The sudden explosion mentioned by João may represent acute fear, such as when we encounter imminent danger.

The slow and insidious corrosion can symbolize chronic fear, which accumulates over time and affects our quality of life.

Hypotheses and Reflections: João may be reflecting on how understanding the components of fear can help control it.

Perhaps he suggests that, just as a chemical engineer unravels a reaction, we should investigate fear to find ways to neutralize it. In summary, João's metaphor invites us to explore fear as a dynamic and multifaceted phenomenon that requires careful analysis to be successfully faced. ✸

André Augusto smiled, but there was a glint of challenge in his eyes. "As a pastor, I see fear as a test of faith. It's when our trust in God is pushed to the limit. Fear drives us to seek spiritual answers, find strength in prayer, and face the unknown with courage."

André Augusto's Perspective: André Augusto, as a pastor, leads us to explore fear through a spiritual lens. Let's enrich the text with facts, emotions, and hypotheses:

Facts about Fear: Fear can be seen as an opportunity for spiritual growth, where our faith is tested.

Trust in God is central to facing fear, as we believe He will guide and protect us.

Emotions Associated with Fear: The challenging glint in André's eyes suggests that he views fear as a chance for overcoming.

Seeking spiritual answers and finding strength in prayer reflects the connection between faith and confronting fear.

Hypotheses and Reflections:

André may be reflecting on how fear can strengthen our relationship with the divine.

Perhaps he encourages others to face the unknown with courage, trusting in God.

In summary, André's perspective invites us to consider fear not only as an emotion but as a spiritual journey that challenges us to grow and trust. ✺

Mário's Metaphor: Mário, the math and physics professor, stood up from his chair. "Fear is like a complex equation, an unknown variable that affects our decisions. We need to solve this internal equation to find inner peace, balancing our fears with rationality." Mário's metaphor, comparing fear to an equation, invites us to explore this emotion from a mathematical perspective. Let's enhance the text with facts, emotions, and hypotheses:

Facts about Fear: Fear is a natural response of our nervous system to perceived threats.
It can influence our choices and behaviors, often unconsciously.
Emotions Associated with Fear: Mário's serious expression suggests that he sees fear as something to be faced seriously.
The search for inner peace indicates that fear can disturb our emotional balance.

Hypotheses and Reflections: Mário may be suggesting that, just as we solve mathematical equations, we should approach fear methodically and analytically. The mentioned rationality could be the key to finding that internal balance.

In summary, Mário invites us to apply mathematical principles to our emotional experience, seeking solutions for the fear equation. ✸

Gérson's Exotic Dish: Gérson, the waiter, served a steaming cup of tea to everyone. "To me, fear is like an exotic dish served in life's restaurant. Sometimes, it's spicy, making us sweat and tremble. Other times, it's sweet and comforting, but it always leaves a lingering taste in our soul." Gérson, with his elegant tray, invites us to savor fear like an exotic dish. Let's explore this intriguing metaphor:

The Exotic Dish: Fear is presented as something rare and unusual, like a dish that piques our curiosity.

The choice of the adjective "exotic" suggests that fear is complex and nuanced.

Flavors of Fear: The spiciness that makes us sweat and tremble represents acute fear, catching us off guard and challenging us.

The sweet and comforting flavor may symbolize fear that leads us to seek refuge, finding solace in our beliefs and relationships.

The Lingering Taste: The taste that remains in the soul suggests that fear leaves lasting marks, even after the moment has passed.

Perhaps the mystery lies in how we handle that taste—whether we savor it or confront it.

Mysterious Hypothesis: Life's restaurant may be a place where we all experience this dish, each with our own recipes and seasonings.

In summary, Gérson invites us to approach fear with curiosity and courage, exploring its different flavors and mysteries. ☄✦

On that night, friends gathered, debating fear under the flickering candlelight. Shadows danced on the walls, as if they had a life of their own, and the wind whispered secrets through the half-opened windows. Each perspective was unique, like notes in a mysterious symphony. ♪♪♪

Fear as an Enigma: Some friends saw fear as an enigma to be deciphered. It hid in the shadows, challenging them to understand its origins and meanings. Hypothesis: Perhaps fear is like an encrypted code, waiting for someone to unravel its secrets. Fear as an Unsettling Companion: Others felt fear as an unsettling companion. It accompanied them in their darkest moments, like a silent presence. Emotion: Loneliness and the feeling of being observed may be associated with this perspective. Fear as a Gateway to the Unknown: Some believed that fear was a portal to the unknown. When faced, it revealed new horizons and challenges. Fact: Fear often drives us to explore what lies beyond our comfort zone. In summary, on that enigmatic night, friends shared their views on fear, creating a dialogue that would echo in each person's memories. ☽✦

Mário's Question about Death: Mário, the math and physics professor, looked at the others and asked, **"What is death to you?"** Mário stood up from his chair, his eyes fixed on his friends. The question about death hung in the air, like a complex equation waiting to be solved. Each person present felt the weight of this inquiry, and shadows danced on the walls, as if whispering long-guarded secrets.

Perspectives on Death:

Santo Agostinho and Serenity: Santo Agostinho, a revered thinker, viewed death as a natural passage. He compared it to a change of state, not an absolute end. According to him, those who have departed are not absent; they are on the other side, just around the corner. Their eyes, filled with glory, still observe us, invisible to our physical eyes.

Death is not the end but a transformation.

Spiritual Vision: Some may see death as a journey to the spiritual world, where we leave material possessions behind and carry only the good we've done for others.

This perspective reminds us that earthly life is just one part of our existence.

The Unknown and Resistance:

Talking about death remains difficult for many. Resistance arises from fear of the unknown and loss of control.

However, facing this question is essential for our mental and emotional well-being.

In summary, death is an enigma, an equation we all try to decipher. It challenges us but also invites reflection on the meaning of life and eternity. ☄✦

Antônio's Contemplative View on Death: Antônio, the doctor, adjusted his glasses with seriousness. "Death is like a final diagnosis. A patient who no longer responds to treatments, a delicate line between life and the unknown. But it's also a mystery, something that transcends our scientific understanding and prompts us to question what exists beyond."

The Final Diagnosis: Antônio compares death to an irrevocable medical diagnosis. When a patient no longer responds to treatments, death presents itself as the inevitable conclusion.

This perspective emphasizes life's finiteness and the fragility of the human body.

The Delicate Line: The "delicate line" between life and the unknown suggests that death is a fragile threshold. It separates us from what we know and launches us into uncharted territory.

This metaphor evokes the idea that death is not merely an end but also a passage to something beyond.

The Unfathomable Mystery: Antônio acknowledges that death transcends our scientific understanding. It remains shrouded in mystery, challenging our certainties and beliefs.

Perhaps it's this mystery that leads us to question what exists beyond earthly life.

In summary, Antônio's view invites us to reflect on death as an enigma that permeates our existence, urging us to seek deeper meanings. ☄✦

João Fernandes, the Chemical Engineer: João Fernandes, the chemical engineer, maintained a steady gaze. "Death is an inevitable chemical reaction. Our bodies break down, much like the elements in a complex formula. But perhaps there is something beyond these reactions, something that eludes our cold analysis."

The Chemical Reaction: João compares death to an unavoidable chemical reaction. Just as elements combine and transform, our bodies also undergo chemical changes when we die.

This perspective emphasizes the intrinsic and universal nature of death.

Beyond the Reactions: The suggestion that "there may be something beyond these reactions" prompts us to question what lies beyond the scope of science.

Perhaps João is pointing to the mystery of consciousness, the soul, or a spiritual dimension.

Cold Analysis and Mystery: "Cold analysis" represents the scientific approach, based on observable facts and evidence.

However, João acknowledges that there are aspects of death that escape this analysis—something that transcends our rational understanding.

In summary, João's view invites us to contemplate death as a complex phenomenon where science and mystery intertwine. ☄✦

André Augusto, the Evangelical Pastor: André Augusto, the evangelical pastor, smiled serenely. "To me, death is a passage. A spiritual journey where we believe in life after death. It's the hope of finding eternal peace, of reuniting with those we love."

The Spiritual Passage: André sees death as a transition, not an absolute end. It leads us from earthly existence to something beyond, like passing through a door.
This perspective is common in many religious traditions, where death is viewed as a change of existence.
Life After Death: Belief in life after death is central for André. He sees death as a door opening to a new dimension, where the soul continues its journey.
This hope comforts us, especially when we face the loss of loved ones.
Reunion with Loved Ones:
The idea of reuniting with those we love after death is comforting. It gives us a sense of continuity and connection beyond this life.
Perhaps this hope enables us to face death with serenity.
In summary, André's view invites us to see death not as an end but as a stage in the soul's spiritual journey.

Gérson, the Waiter's Metaphor: Gérson, the waiter, carefully cleaned the dishes as his words hung in the air like the aroma of a freshly served dish. The metaphor of death as an unexpected dish in the restaurant of existence invites us to explore this universal experience:

Variety of Flavors: Death, like a dish, can have different flavors. Sometimes it's bitter and hard to swallow, like an indigestible meal. Other times, it's sweet and comforting, like a delicacy that warms the soul.
This duality reflects the complexity of death and how it uniquely affects each of us.
Sharing the Banquet: The idea that we all share this death banquet transcends cultures, beliefs, and personal tastes.
Regardless of our individual preferences, we all face this common experience.

The Mystery of the Restaurant of Existence: he restaurant of existence is a mysterious place where dishes are served without prior notice. We don't choose what's presented to us.

Perhaps the secret lies in how we appreciate each dish, even when the flavor is unknown.

In summary, Gérson invites us to reflect on death as an intrinsic part of our journey—a dish we all share, regardless of our preferences and ages. ☄✦

On that enigmatic night, friends shared their views on death, creating a dialogue that would echo in each person's memories. The concept of death was explored from various angles, revealing unique perspectives:

Death as an Enigma: Some friends saw death as a puzzle to be deciphered. It hid in the shadows, challenging them to understand its origins and meanings.

Hypothesis: Perhaps death is like an encrypted code, waiting for someone to unveil its secrets.

Emotion: Loneliness and the feeling of being observed may be associated with this perspective.

Death as an Unsettling Companion: Others felt death as an unsettling companion. It accompanied them in their darkest moments, like a silent presence.

This perspective acknowledges the weight of mortality and its constant presence.

Death as a Portal to the Unknown: Some believed that death was a gateway to the unknown. When faced, it revealed new horizons and challenges.

Fact: Death often compels us to explore what lies beyond our comfort zones.

In summary, that enigmatic night allowed friends to share their unique visions of death, weaving a rich tapestry of perspectives that would resonate in their memories. ☽✦

Regarding cultural perspectives on death and the afterlife, different societies worldwide offer diverse interpretations:

African Culture: Transition to Another Reality:
Many African societies view death not as the end but as a transition to another realm.
Funeral rituals often carry religious significance, shaping how individuals and communities cope with loss and grief.
Western Culture: Emphasis on Finality:

In Western societies, death is often seen as final, emphasizing biological aspects and individual legacies.

Asian Culture: Spirituality and Impermanence:

In Japan, Buddhist funerals blend spirituality with ceremony, underscoring life's impermanence and the soul's journey after physical death.

Diasporic Influences: Enriching Understanding:

Diasporic communities merge cultural legacies from their homelands with their new surroundings, creating hybrid perceptions of death.

In summary, death is a multifaceted topic, reflecting diverse beliefs and values across cultures. □□□□

Antônio, the doctor, looked at the others and asked, **"What does politics mean to you?"**

As for politics, it encompasses citizens' engagement in public affairs through opinions and voting. The term originates from the Greek word "polis," meaning "city." In ancient Greek city-states, politics regulated coexistence among inhabitants and neighboring city-states. Beyond political parties and institutions, politics involves associations, unions, protests, and active citizen participation. Public policies emerge when governments address specific societal issues, seeking solutions through analysis and evaluation. Citizen participation is essential for addressing civil society's challenges, making politics a vital tool for organizing and improving community life. ☐

João Fernandes, the Chemical Engineer: João Fernandes, the chemical engineer, leaned forward as if about to reveal a long-guarded secret. "Politics… Ah, my friends, politics is like a complex chemical reaction. It unfolds behind the scenes, involving different elements, interests, and agendas. Sometimes, it's explosive, like an unstable compound threatening to detonate at any moment. Other times, it's slow and corrosive, like an acid silently eroding the foundations of society."

Political Explosion: The comparison to an unstable compound suggests that politics can be volatile and unpredictable.

When interests collide, politics can explode into heated debates, protests, and abrupt changes.

Silent Corrosion: The analogy to a silently corroding acid highlights the gradual influence of politics.

Slow and persistent policies can shape society over time, often without fanfare.

Elements and Agendas: Politics involves different elements, such as parties, ideologies, and individuals.

Political agendas vary, with each group seeking to promote its interests.

In summary, politics is a powerful force capable of transforming societies and shaping the course of history. □

André Augusto, the Evangelical Pastor: André Augusto, the evangelical pastor, smiled, but there was a shadow in his eyes. "To me, politics is an incessant quest for harmony in human coexistence. Just like in faith, we need to find consensus to live in peace. But, my friends, there's something more… something hidden between the lines of laws and speeches. A hidden force that shapes destinies."

Harmony in Coexistence: André sees politics as a search for harmony among people. It aims to create an environment where different interests coexist peacefully.
The comparison to faith suggests that both fields seek balance and healthy coexistence.
Consensus and Peace: The need to find consensus reflects the importance of politics in collective decision-making.
Peace is the ultimate goal, and politics is a tool to achieve it.
The Hidden Force: The allusion to a "hidden force" in the lines of laws and speeches suggests that politics goes beyond the visible.
Perhaps this force relates to the influence of power structures or underlying social dynamics.
In summary, André invites us to reflect on politics not only as a formal process but as something permeating our existence, shaping our collective destiny. ☐

Mário, the Math and Physics Professor: Mário traced invisible formulas in the air, as if deciphering an enigma. "Politics is like a system of interconnected equations. We need to balance interests, resolve conflicts, and find optimal solutions for everyone. But sometimes, these equations have unknown variables, invisible forces that distort the results."

Interconnected Equations: The analogy to a system of equations highlights the complexity of politics.
Just as in equations, political interests are interconnected, and their solutions affect one another.
Balancing Interests: The quest for balance reflects the need to consider multiple factors when making political decisions.
Resolving conflicts requires finding solutions that benefit society as a whole.
Unknown Variables and Invisible Forces:
The unknown variables may represent hidden influences, such as undisclosed interests or backstage powers.

These invisible forces can distort political outcomes, affecting the equation unpredictably.

In summary, politics is a dynamic system where complex equations intertwine, and finding solutions requires skill and sensitivity to deal with unknown variables.

Gérson, the Waiter's Metaphor: Gérson, the waiter, served red wine, his eyes shining with an unusual intensity. "Politics is like a sophisticated dish in the restaurant of life. Sometimes bitter, like a fierce power struggle, other times sweet, like a successful agreement. But, my friends, beware of what's on the menu. Not everything is as it seems."

Sophisticated Dish: Politics is compared to a sophisticated dish, suggesting complexity and refinement.

Like an exquisite dish, politics involves nuances and varied flavors.

Bitterness of Struggle: The fierce power struggle can be bitter, akin to a challenging taste.

Politics often involves rivalries and conflicting interests.

Sweetness of Agreement: A successful agreement is sweet, bringing harmony and resolution.

Politics can also lead to positive outcomes when parties find common ground.

Beware of the Menu: Gérson's warning reminds us that not everything is as it appears in politics.

Sometimes hidden agendas and undisclosed interests lie behind the surface.

In summary, politics is a complex dish with nuances of bitterness and sweetness, and we must be attentive to our choices from life's menu. □

That night, friends gathered and, under the flickering candlelight, debated the political enigma. The maps on the walls seemed to whisper secrets, and the curtains shimmered as if concealing answers in the shadows. Each perspective was unique, like notes in a mysterious symphony. □✦

Gérson, the waiter, looked at the others and asked, **"What does socialization mean to you?"**

Socialization: Socialization is the process by which individuals learn the way of life, habits, and customs of a society. Its objectives include teaching individuals the norms and values of a culture and defining their sense of belonging within the social world. In sociology, socialization is crucial for integrating individuals into a group and developing social skills. It occurs from childhood to adulthood, shaping our identity and behavior. Through socialization, we learn to adapt to existing cultural patterns in society, acquiring the habits that enable us to live in community. However, it's essential to remember that not everything is as it seems: hidden forces and interests influence our socialization process behind the appearances. ☐

Antônio, the Doctor's Analogy: Antônio rested his chin on his hand, as if contemplating a crucial diagnosis. "Socialization is like a thorough clinical examination. We observe symptoms, interactions, and connections among people. It's vital for our mental and emotional health, like medicine that keeps us balanced."

Clinical Examination: The comparison to a clinical examination highlights the importance of socialization.

Just as a doctor assesses physical symptoms, socialization helps us understand social and emotional dynamics.

Observing Symptoms and Interactions:

Observing social symptoms involves noticing how people behave, communicate, and interact.

This analysis helps us comprehend human relationships and our own adaptation.

Mental and Emotional Health: Socialization acts as medicine for our mental and emotional well-being.

It connects us, combats isolation, and promotes overall wellness.

In summary, like an attentive doctor, we should examine and care for our social interactions to maintain emotional balance. ☐

João Fernandes, the Chemical Engineer: João Fernandes, the chemical engineer, stirred the sugar in his coffee, his eyes searching for something beyond words. "Socialization is a chemical reaction between individuals. Sometimes, it's explosive, like when we meet someone we're attracted to, and our emotional molecules collide. Other times, it's stable, like a lasting friendship, a bond that strengthens over time."

Chemical Reaction: The comparison to a chemical reaction highlights the dynamic nature of socialization.

Just like in chemical reactions, social interactions can be unpredictable and vary in intensity.

Emotional Explosion: Emotional explosion occurs when our "emotional molecules" collide forcefully.

This can happen when we meet someone special or fall in love.

Stability of Friendship: A lasting friendship is like a stable bond that strengthens over time.

This stability is essential for our emotional well-being.

In summary, socialization is a complex dance of emotions and connections, shaping our relationships and experiences throughout life. □

André Augusto, the Evangelical Pastor: André Augusto smiled, as if seeing beyond the visible. "As a religious leader, I view socialization as an opportunity to share faith and hope. It's when we connect spiritually, when our souls touch and find purpose."

Sharing Faith and Hope: André sees socialization as a means to spread faith and hope.
Connecting with others can strengthen our spirituality and provide meaning.
Souls Touching:

The idea that our souls touch suggests a deep and transcendent connection. Socialization allows us to find people with whom we share spiritual affinities.

Finding Purpose: Purpose is discovered through relating to others and contributing to something greater.

Socialization helps us uncover our role in the community and the world.

In summary, socialization is a spiritual journey where our souls intertwine, finding meaning through connection with others. ☐

Mário, the Math and Physics Professor: Mário traced invisible equations in the air, as if deciphering a code. "Socialization is like a dynamic system. Variables come and go, influencing our lives. We need to find the right balance, like a well-adjusted equation that keeps us moving."

Dynamic System: The comparison to a dynamic system highlights the ever-changing nature of socialization.

Just as variables in equations, social interactions affect our lives.

Finding Balance: Striving for balance is essential in socialization.

Finding the right point between social connections and personal time is like adjusting an equation.

Well-Adjusted Equation: A well-adjusted equation keeps us moving, just as healthy social relationships propel us forward.

Balance is crucial for our well-being. In summary, socialization is a constant dance of variables, where we find our rhythm and equilibrium to move ahead. □

That night, coffee cups exuded scents of shared conversations and secrets, while friends explored the mysteries of socialization. □✦

André Augusto, the Evangelical Pastor: André Augusto, the evangelical pastor, looked at the others and asked, **"What is capitalism to you?"** Capitalism is an economic and social system based on private ownership, profit, and capital accumulation. It originated during the transition from the Middle Ages to the Modern Age when the bourgeoisie emerged as a new social class. Some characteristics of capitalism include free enterprise, competition, supply and demand, profit as the primary production goal, and the possibility of accumulating wealth. ✹

Historically, capitalism has gone through three phases:

Commercial Capitalism (Mercantilism): This phase emerged during the transition from the Middle Ages to the Modern Age. It was characterized by trade, commerce, and the accumulation of wealth through overseas exploration and colonization.

Industrial Capitalism (Industrial Revolution): The Industrial Revolution marked a significant shift as mechanization and factory-based production transformed economies. Capitalism became closely tied to industrialization, technological advancements, and urbanization.

Financial Capitalism (Monopoly Capitalism): In this phase, financial institutions gained prominence. Monopolies and large corporations dominated markets, and financial speculation played a crucial role. The concentration of economic power increased, leading to debates about economic inequality and corporate influence.

Each phase brought substantial changes in how economies and societies functioned. ☽✦

Antônio, the Doctor's Analogy: Antônio adjusted his glasses, and silence hung over the table. "Capitalism is like a clinical diagnosis. It's based on private property, profit, and capital accumulation. Similar to medicine, it seeks to understand symptoms and treatments for economic well-being." ✸ Indeed, capitalism shares similarities with a clinical diagnosis. Let's explore more details about this economic system:

Private Property: In capitalism, private property is fundamental. Individuals and companies own assets, resources, and means of production. This ownership forms the basis for wealth generation and economic decision-making.

Profit and Capital Accumulation: The central goal of capitalism is profit. Companies aim to maximize earnings through the production and sale of goods and services. Capital accumulation occurs when profits are reinvested to expand businesses or acquire more assets.

Economic Symptoms and Treatments: Like in medicine, capitalism requires diagnosis and treatment. We assess economic indicators such as GDP growth, inflation, and unemployment. Economic policies, such as fiscal and monetary adjustments, serve as the "treatments" to maintain economic well-being. In summary, capitalism is a complex system with its own "ailments" and "remedies," shaping our society and economy. ✸

André Augusto, the Evangelical Pastor's Spiritual Perspective: André Augusto smiled, but there was something enigmatic in his gaze. "I see capitalism as a spiritual journey. Like faith, it involves choices, values, and a quest for prosperity. Private property is like a divine gift, yet it also conceals dark secrets."

Spiritual Journey: André's view invites us to consider capitalism beyond mere economics—a spiritual journey.

Dual Nature of Private Property: Private property is compared to a divine gift granted to us. However, it also harbors dark secrets, such as inequalities and exploitation.

Reflections on Values: Perhaps André suggests that, like in faith, we should reflect on our values and how they manifest in the economic context. In summary, André encourages us to explore capitalism not only as an economic system but as a journey transcending material concerns, prompting us to question our societal role. ✹

Mário, the Math and Physics Professor's Mathematical Analogy: Mário traced invisible equations in the air, as if deciphering a hidden code. "Capitalism is a system of complex equations. Supply and demand, profit and investment. We must find balance for society to function, but there are unknown variables that elude us."

Complex Equations: The comparison to equations highlights capitalism's intricate nature.

Interconnected Variables: Supply and demand, profit and investment are interconnected variables.

Seeking Balance: Balance is essential for societal functioning.

Hidden Variables: These variables may be dark secrets or unpredictable factors. Like mathematics, capitalism involves mysteries waiting to be unraveled. In summary, capitalism is an ever-evolving equation where finding balance is crucial for societal well-being. ✹

Gérson, the Waiter's Enigma: Gérson, the waiter, served the red wine with an elegant gesture, and his low voice echoed through the hall like an unsolved enigma. The room was saturated with whispered conversations and muffled laughter, but his words cut through the air with clarity.

Capitalism:

"Capitalism," he began, "is like a sophisticated being that permeates the world and our lives. Sometimes, it reveals itself as cruel, like an economic crisis that suffocates us, leaving us with no way out. Other times, it is generous, like a heated market that intoxicates us with opportunities and wealth."

Gérson paused, gazing at the invisible horizon. "We all share this global relationship with capitalism, but who ultimately holds the true power? Corporate magnates? Governments? Or perhaps the system itself is an autonomous entity, guiding us like invisible marionettes?"

He leaned a little closer, as if sharing a secret. "Perhaps capital lies in the hands of those who understand its intrinsic nature, who play the game masterfully and manipulate the rules in their favor. Or maybe it rests with dreamers, visionaries seeking a more equitable redistribution."

Gérson smiled mysteriously. "Who holds capital? The answer is in constant flux, like market waves. But one thing is certain: the enigma persists, and we mere mortals continue to unravel it, glass after glass."

André Augusto, the Evangelical Pastor's Perspective: André Augusto fixed his gaze on the audience and posed the question: **"What is family to you?"** Silence hung in the room, as if everyone were reflecting on something deep and personal.

Family:

"A family," he began, "is more than blood ties or cohabitation under the same roof. It is a refuge, a safe harbor where we find love, support, and belonging."

André looked at his hands, searching for the right words. "For some, family is a traditional nucleus—parents and children. For others, it extends beyond blood, including friends, mentors, and even pets."

He smiled, recalling stories shared in his congregation. "There are families that face challenges but remain united, like an unshakable fortress. And there are those formed by choice—bonds of friendship and solidarity."

"Yet," André continued, "family remains a mystery. Sometimes, we forge deep connections with unexpected people. Perhaps it's divine intervention, God's hand weaving our destinies."

He concluded with hope. "Regardless of its form, family is a precious gift. It teaches us about love, forgiveness, and resilience. Ultimately, it's where we find our true home."

Antônio, the Doctor's Analogy: Antônio adjusted his glasses, and his voice took on a serious tone. "A family is like a clinical diagnosis," he began, "where we observe symptoms of love, care, and connection. It's vital for our emotional health and well-being, but it also conceals old wounds and buried secrets."

Emotional Scars: "Emotional scars, often invisible, are as real as physical ones," Antônio explained. "Each family member carries their own burden—untold stories, fears, and hopes."

Hidden Secrets: "And then there are secrets," he continued. "Sometimes small omissions, other times painful truths we'd rather avoid. Yet these secrets shape our family dynamics, like pieces of a complex puzzle."

Antônio paused, reflecting. "Perhaps the true art lies in balancing the delicate dance between love and vulnerability. Accepting imperfections, forgiving flaws, while protecting the bonds that unite us."

"A family," he concluded, "is an ever-evolving diagnosis. And, much like in medicine, treatment requires patience, understanding, and generous doses of love."

João Fernandes, the Chemical Engineer: João Fernandes leaned forward, as if sharing a forbidden formula. "A family is a chemical reaction between kindred souls," he began, "a complex experiment that occurs in our hearts and minds. Sometimes, it's explosive, like heated arguments that leave emotional scars, akin to corrosive acids."

Stability and Bonds: "Other times," João continued, "it's stable, like the bond between parents and children that transcends time. This connection, like a strong covalent bond, holds the family structure together even when we face storms and adverse reactions."

Unknown Variables: "But," João added, "much like in chemistry, there are unknown variables. Sometimes, the elements don't fit perfectly, and the reaction doesn't occur as expected. And, like good scientists, we need to adjust conditions, find the right balance, and allow the family to evolve."

He smiled mysteriously. "Perhaps the secret lies in understanding that there's no universal formula for family. Each combination is unique, with its own products and byproducts. Ultimately, family is our own alchemy, transforming the ordinary into something extraordinary."

Mário, the Math and Physics Professor: Mário traced invisible equations in the air, as if deciphering an ancient enigma. "A family is a dynamic system," he began, "where variables enter and exit, influencing our lives. Much like in mathematics, we must find the right balance."

Insoluble Equations: "But there are insoluble equations that challenge us," Mário continued. "Questions without definitive answers, like the quest for perfect harmony among family members. Sometimes, the variables don't align, and the solution remains elusive."

Universal Laws: "However," Mário reflected, "much like in physics, family also follows universal laws. Love is a constant, patience acts as a gravitational force that keeps us together, and time is an inexorable variable."

He smiled thoughtfully. "Perhaps the true family equation lies in accepting that not everything can be solved. Sometimes, beauty resides in imperfection, in the unknowns that challenge us to grow and evolve together."

Gérson, the waiter, served a glass of water, and his gaze wandered to the horizon. "A family is like something special in our lives," he began, "sometimes we have disagreements that eat away at us and affect our emotions. Other times, we have good moments, like shared memories that make us happy, reminiscing about past events. We all play a part in these memories, but who is the invisible entity that watches over our destinies?"

Perhaps we will never know, or perhaps, after we depart from this world, the answers will reveal themselves. Life is full of mysteries, and destiny often remains hidden, like an enigma that challenges our understanding. What we can do is live with curiosity, accepting uncertainty and exploring the paths that unfold. □□□

And as the candles flickered, friends explored the mysteries of family like archaeologists unearthing ancestral secrets.

João Fernandes, the chemical engineer, looked at the others and proposed a challenge: **each person should share their thoughts on astrology**.

João Fernandes (Chemical Engineer): His eyes sparkled like distant stars. "Astrology is like the chemical composition of the stars. Each zodiac sign is akin to an element in the celestial periodic table. Planets, like atoms, mysteriously influence our lives. We are cosmic dust dancing to the constellations' tune."

Antônio (Doctor): For him, astrology resembled a medical diagnosis, revealing hidden patterns. However, unlike medicine, there's no prescription for cure.

André Augusto (Evangelical Pastor): André Augusto views astrology as divine signs written in the stars. The magi followed a star to the birth of Jesus, suggesting that there is more to this mystery than science.

Mário (Math and Physics Professor): With his analytical gaze, Mário compares astrology to a cosmic equation. Planets are variables that influence our lives. However, his scientific skepticism remains.

Gérson (Restaurant Waiter): Always observant, Gérson likens astrology to a restaurant menu. Each zodiac sign has its special dish, and the universe holds surprises.

Mário, the Math and Physics Professor, proposes a challenge: **Each person should share what they consider luck**.

Mário (Math and Physics Professor): He looks at the group with an enigmatic smile and says, "Luck is like a nonlinear equation. Sometimes, variables align perfectly, and everything works out. But as a scientist, I know there's more than chance involved."

Antônio (Doctor): Antônio, drawing from his clinical experience, responds, "To me, luck is when a difficult diagnosis resolves. It's like finding a needle in the haystack of health. Luck lies in the precision of treatment."

João Fernandes (Chemical Engineer): João, with his analytical mind, states, "Luck is like an unexpected chemical reaction. Sometimes, elements combine surprisingly. Life is a series of experiments."

André Augusto (Evangelical Pastor): André reflects, "Luck is God's hand guiding our steps. As a religious leader, I see divine signs in every event. Luck is a blessing."

Gérson (Restaurant Waiter): Ever observant, Gérson smiles and says, "Luck is when a customer orders the daily special, and I still have the ingredients. It's like winning the culinary lottery."

And so, that night, friends debated the enigma of capitalism, socialization, and family. The steam from their cups flickered, as if containing secrets waiting to be revealed.

As rain tapped on the mansion's windows, friends shared their perspectives on luck. The web of the enigma extended, connecting their views and experiences.

Since I'm part of your discussion, I'll propose a topic as well: **What does love mean to you?**

Love is a complex and multifaceted concept that can be interpreted differently depending on each person's perspective. Here are some possible interpretations from these four fictional individuals:

Antônio (Doctor): For Antônio, love can be seen as a biological phenomenon—a powerful force that binds people and has profound effects on physical and mental health. He might mention the release of hormones like oxytocin and dopamine that occur when we're in love.

João Fernandes (Chemical Engineer): João might view love as a complex chemical reaction. He could compare love to a catalytic process that accelerates and intensifies emotions and feelings.

André Augusto (Evangelical Pastor): André might understand love as a divine gift, a commandment from God to love others as ourselves. He could refer to biblical passages that speak about love and compassion.

Mário (Math and Physics Professor): Mário could see love through the lens of logic and set theory, where love is the intersection of feelings, emotions, and shared experiences between two people. He might also view love as a fundamental force, akin to the fundamental forces of physics.

Gérson: Hmm, this is more challenging. But I think love can truly be understood as a combination of sensations and emotions processed in our brains. However, love is often described as a deeply personal and subjective experience that can vary greatly from person to person. Some may describe love in terms of a deep, lasting connection with another person, while others may see it as a feeling of joy and happiness. Ultimately, love can be a complex blend of emotions, behaviors, and beliefs associated with strong affection for someone else.

Mário: Congratulations, Gérson, you provided a logical answer, but in my view, it lacked tacit knowledge in this area. I apologize to everyone, but I have to attend other tables, so until next time, gentlemen, said Gérson before disappearing from view.

After a few more rounds, the four friends decided to leave. Mario shouted, "Gérson, please bring the check," but a different Gérson came to the table. "Gentlemen, would you like anything else?" he asked. Antônio looked at him and asked, "Where's Gerson?" The waiter replied, "I apologize for the confusion, gentlemen, but there is no waiter by that name working here."

Antônio looked surprised at his friends and said, "That's strange. I'm sure his name was Gérson. Anyway, let's settle the bill and leave. It seems we had an interesting night!" They laughed together, paid the bill, and left the bar, still trying to understand the confusion with the waiter's name.

As the four friends exited the bar, laughing and chatting, they didn't notice the strange look from the waiter who observed them. He stood there, with an intrigued expression on his face, watching them as they walked away. Perhaps he was pondering the mix-up with the name Gérson, or maybe there was something else on his mind. Either way, the night had certainly been an adventure for all of them.

The end.